What Works! Successful Strategies for Pursuing National Board Certification Version 3.1

What Works! Successful Strategies for Pursuing National Board Certification Version 3.1

Components 1 and 2

Second Edition

Bobbie Faulkner

BLOOMSBURY ACADEMIC
NEW YORK • LONDON • OXFORD • NEW DELHI • SYDNEY

BLOOMSBURY ACADEMIC

Bloomsbury Publishing Inc, 1359 Broadway, New York, NY 10018, USA
Bloomsbury Publishing Plc, 50 Bedford Square, London, WC1B 3DP, UK
Bloomsbury Publishing Ireland, 29 Earlsfort Terrace, Dublin 2, D02 AY28, Ireland

BLOOMSBURY, BLOOMSBURY ACADEMIC and the Diana logo are trademarks of Bloomsbury Publishing Plc

First published in the United States of America 2026

Copyright © Bloomsbury Publishing Inc, 2026

Cover image: © istock/Sensay

All rights reserved. No part of this publication may be: i) reproduced or transmitted in any form, electronic or mechanical, including photocopying, recording or by means of any information storage or retrieval system without prior permission in writing from the publishers; or ii) used or reproduced in any way for the training, development or operation of artificial intelligence (AI) technologies, including generative AI technologies. The rights holders expressly reserve this publication from the text and data mining exception as per Article 4(3) of the Digital Single Market Directive (EU) 2019/790.

Bloomsbury Publishing Inc does not have any control over, or responsibility for, any third-party websites referred to or in this book. All internet addresses given in this book were correct at the time of going to press. The author and publisher regret any inconvenience caused if addresses have changed or sites have ceased to exist, but can accept no responsibility for any such changes.

A catalog record for this book is available from the Library of Congress

ISBN: HB: 978-1-4758-7513-3
Pbk: 978-1-4758-7514-0
ePDF: 978-1-4758-7515-7
eBook: 979-8-7651-6490-7

Typeset by Deanta Global Publishing Services, Chennai, India
Printed and bound in the United States of America

For product safety related questions contact productsafety@bloomsbury.com.

To find out more about our authors and books visit www.bloomsbury.com and sign up for our newsletters.

Contents

Preface vi
Acknowledgments vii

Introduction 1

1 What Is National Board Certification? 3

2 Building Your Foundation 7

3 Getting Started and Getting Support 13

4 Component 1 Content Knowledge: A Computer-Based Assessment of Content and Pedagogical Knowledge 21

5 Component 2 Differentiation in Instruction: Sharing Accomplished Teaching through Student Work Samples 33

6 Writing for the National Board 49

7 Understanding Your Scores 65

Appendix A: SSTARS Lesson Plan Template Based on the Architecture of Accomplished Teaching 69
Appendix B: Sentence Stems for Analytic and Reflective Writing 70
Appendix C: Ten Editing Tips to Trim Space without Trimming Content 71
About the Author 72

Preface

This publication is written to support candidates doing Components 1 and/or 2 of the current Version 3.1 of the National Board Certification process. While the content of Components 1 and 2 hasn't changed since its final rollout in 2016, National Board Certified Teachers (NBCTs) have gained knowledge and experience useful to candidates pursuing certification. This volume reflects such collective knowledge.

Acknowledgments

I would like to offer special thanks to those who have contributed significantly to my personal National Board Certification journey. From Scottsdale, I will always owe appreciation to Nancy Creighton Brown, former Career Ladder Specialist whose open mind, vision, and dedication to Scottsdale teachers allowed National Board Certification to take root and grow in Scottsdale.

Also influential in my continuing journey is the core group of Scottsdale Professional Learning Facilitators: Susan Leonard, Abbey Bobbitt, Anne Waddington, and Tammy Dias. Certification opened leadership opportunities with groups such as the Stanford University National Board Resource Center and the Region 10 Texas National Board Candidate Cohorts.

A personal thank you goes to my husband, Jim, who has supported all my National Board endeavors, which includes many hours in front of the computer. Finally, the staff of the National Board under the leadership of Dr. Peggy Brookins deserves recognition for being responsive to the needs of National Board candidates.

Introduction

The *What Works!* book series for National Board candidates began with an off-the-cuff remark. "You ought to write a book," a fellow Candidate Support Provider (CSP) said one day after a workshop for candidates. So that's what I did. This publication is actually the fifth in the *What Works!* series, and the second to address the revised 3.0 version.

What Works! Successful Strategies for Pursuing National Board Certification Version 3.1, Components 1 and 2 joins its companion book about Components 1 and 2, and replaces all earlier versions of the series.

What Works! Successful Strategies for Pursuing National Board Certification Version 3.1, Components 1 and 2 is not endorsed by the NBPTS or anyone involved in the National Board Certification process. It's not meant to be a "Cliff Notes" type of publication one can use to circumvent the NBPTS documents and instructions.

What Works! Successful Strategies for Pursuing National Board Certification Version 3.1, Components 1 and 2 contains tips, opinions, information, documents, and examples that have been created solely for the purposes of demonstration and are neither approved nor endorsed by the NBPTS. Keep in mind that

- The author is not a trained assessor and does not imply that any sample writing would score well and/or lead to certification according to the NBPTS Scoring Rubrics.
- All samples are hypothetical, fabricated, made up, and are not from actual candidate writing. They cannot be copied for use within a component.
- *What Works! Successful Strategies for Pursuing National Board Certification, Version 3.1, Components 1 and 2* is as current as I can make it. However, it is the responsibility of the candidate to be fully informed of the current NBPTS requirements in case directions change after the book's publication.

This update is a labor of love for my fellow educators and National Board candidates. It is my hope that the information will make your journey toward National Board Certification just a little easier, more meaningful, and successful.

1 What Is National Board Certification?

Six-Word Memoir: Know Your Standards. Know Them Well!
BRITNEY, NC

NBPTS Background and History

National Board Certification is a national *voluntary* system that certifies teachers who meet a set of high and rigorous Standards for what accomplished teachers should know and be able to do. This certification system was developed by the National Board for Professional Teaching Standards (NBPTS) and put in place in 1987 following recommendations from the Carnegie reports *A Nation at Risk* and *A Nation Prepared*.

The National Board has developed high, rigorous, research-based Standards to measure the effectiveness of a teacher's practice. Teachers complete a series of written exercises that probe the depth of their knowledge of their subject matter. The process involves an extensive series of performance-based assessments that include

- Teaching portfolios
- Student work samples
- Written commentaries
- Videos
- Analysis of the teacher's classroom practice and the impact on student learning.

The work is based on long-established research that identifies and recognizes sound educational practices that result in student learning. The NBPTS has commissioned more than 140 studies and papers on the value of the certification process as well as its Standards and assessment. The process has also been validated by a number of independent studies.

The Five Core Propositions

The Core Propositions are the heart of the National Board process. They outline the expectations and values for what *accomplished* teachers should know and be able to do, and are the umbrella under which the other elements of the National Board Certification process are organized. Accomplished teaching implies going *above and beyond* what is typically expected of the average teacher. The Propositions describe skills in the following areas:

Proposition 1: Commitment to Students

- Accomplished teachers know the developmental levels of their students, believe that all students can learn regardless of background, and use their knowledge to design effective instruction for all students and a variety of learning styles.

Proposition 2: Knowledge of Subject

- Building upon their knowledge of students, accomplished teachers advance their own understanding of their content area and develop a wide range of strategies to set high and worthwhile goals to teach that subject matter to their students.

Proposition 3: Manage and Monitor Student Learning

- Accomplished teachers understand how to manage, motivate, monitor, and assess student learning by planning appropriate learning sequences to achieve the desired outcomes and adjusting instruction as needed. Accomplished teachers also know how to structure the learning environment for optimum learning.

Proposition 4: Think Systematically about Their Teaching and Learn from Experience

- Accomplished teachers analyze student learning and reflect on their teaching practice. They then determine the next set of high and worthwhile goals, implement appropriate instruction, and continue the analysis and reflection cycle.

Proposition 5: Teachers Are Members of Learning Communities

- Accomplished teachers collaborate with other professionals, parents, and their larger community to support and enhance student learning.

The National Board Standards

There are twenty-five certificates that cover many subject areas and student development levels. Each contains a set of Standards, which, along with the Five Core Propositions, form the foundation of National Board Certification. The Standards identify specific knowledge, skills, and attitudes that support accomplished practice, while emphasizing the holistic nature of teaching. They identify how a teacher's professional judgment is reflected in action and they reflect the Five Core Propositions. They identify what an accomplished teacher should know and be able to do.

To achieve National Board Certification and be considered an accomplished teacher, a candidate must show *clear, convincing, and consistent evidence that his or her teaching practice reflects the Standards*. Understanding the Standards and how to demonstrate them in practice provides evidence of accomplished teaching.

What Works! Understanding Your Standards

- *Read* the Standards multiple times. Pay attention to the examples included in each.
- *Think* about how you already incorporate the Standards in your teaching.
- *Highlight* things you already do regularly in one color, things you do sometimes in a second color, and things you rarely or never do in a third color. This will help you recognize your strengths and what areas might be bolstered in your practice.
- *Show* clear, consistent, convincing evidence that your teaching is based on the National Board Standards.

WHY IT WORKS! The Standards were developed to identify accomplished teaching. Candidates are expected to show evidence of the Standards in their teaching.

The Process

National Board Certification is a rigorous process that may take up to five years to achieve. Candidates are asked to:

- *Demonstrate* within their teaching practice the rigorous Standards discussed above.
- *Show* leadership, collaboration, learning, reflective practice, and professionalism.
- *Prepare* a portfolio of three written entries that document their teaching practice.
- *Focus* on the analysis of student work samples, classroom practice and professional development, collaboration and leadership.
- *Make* videos of the teacher working with his/her class.
- *Complete* a series of subject-specific computer tests at an Assessment Center to document knowledge of their content area.

National Board Certification is the highest, most comprehensive voluntary professional development experience available to teachers. Examining their teaching practice and professional accomplishments in depth provides teachers with a professional growth experience unlike any other.

2 Building Your Foundation

You know you are a National Board Candidate when your idea of summer reading is poring over grade level teaching manuals for the Assessment Center instead of enjoying juicy romance novels.
ROSEMARY

Who Is an Accomplished Teacher?

In a nutshell, an accomplished teacher is one who goes *above and beyond* what is typically expected. Accomplished teachers practice exceptional, skilled teaching. They have a strong knowledge base of subject matter and pedagogy, demonstrate complex, nuanced professional work, and consistently meet rigorous Standards of practice. Above all, accomplished teachers are committed to their students, know their subjects and how to teach them, know how to manage and monitor student learning, reflect on their practice and learn from their experience, and are learners, collaborators, and leaders within their professional communities.

Accomplished teachers are teachers just like you, who try their best every day to meet their students' needs, keep current with pedagogy and subject knowledge, and work with others in their schools and districts to create an environment conducive to supporting the healthy growth and development of their students, academically, socially, and emotionally.

What Is Accomplished Teaching?

Accomplished teaching is the entwined double helix of knowing your subject and how to teach it, as shown in the Architecture of Accomplished Teaching graphic. The two strands are closely interwoven and almost seamlessly connected. Accomplished teaching combines both the art and craft of teaching along with a solid knowledge base of content and child development.

Accomplished teaching means planning and demonstrating effective instruction for *these students, at this time, in this place*. The National Board describes accomplished teaching practices in the Standards developed for each certificate. They are the specific teaching behaviors that accomplished teachers demonstrate within their teaching practice. As a candidate for National Board Certification, you need to show evidence of the National Board Standards in your teaching practice.

The Architecture of Accomplished Teaching

The Architecture of Accomplished Teaching (AAT) is the National Board version of an accomplished lesson/unit plan. It's a double helix representation of accomplished teaching practice as it applies to the lessons candidates use in their entries and in assessment center exercises. It is designed to give a visual representation of how the accomplished teaching of units of study and lessons are organized. It is an under-used tool that can add greatly to the understanding of the National Board process and what the National Board is "looking for." You can find it in the General Portfolio Instructions document and in the "What Teachers Should Know and Do" booklet found in the HOMEROOM section of the NB website. Many prompts you'll respond to in your Written Commentaries are connected to specific steps on the AAT.

Candidates often lament that if they just knew what the National Board "wanted," they'd know what to do for each component. In truth, candidates who understand the Architecture of Accomplished Teaching and use its structure as the basis for planning their lesson sequences will demonstrate what the assessors want—evidence of accomplished teaching. I suggest posting a copy of it near your computer for frequent and easy reference.

What Works! Studying the Architecture of Accomplished Teaching—from the bottom up.

Step 1—Start with knowledge of your students. *(Proposition 1)*

- Who are they? Where are they now in their learning? Where should you begin?
- What knowledge about your students influenced the goals you set?
- How do you incorporate this knowledge into your lesson planning?
- What will success for your students look like?

Step 2—Continue setting high, worthwhile goals. *(Proposition 2)*

- How do the goals you set connect to your Standards and portfolio instructions?
- How do the goals fit into the sequence of your overarching goals?
- What do you want your students to know at the end of the lesson or unit?

Step 3—Implement Instruction. *(Proposition 3)*

- What approaches/strategies do you plan to use to accomplish your goals?
- In what sequence might you plan the strategies you plan to use?
- How will the strategies you choose support your students' learning?
- What is your rationale for implementing instruction this way?
- What criteria might you use to decide if and when to use another strategy?

Step 4—Evaluate Student Learning. *(Proposition 4)*

- How will you assess student learning?
- Why did you choose these methods for these students at this time, in this setting?
- What evidence will let you know that the instruction was successful—or not?
- What, if anything, did the assessment(s) tell you about your instruction?
- Where will you go next?

Step 5—Reflect on the effectiveness of your lesson design and decisions. *(Proposition 5)*

- How do you know whether you made the right choices?
- What was successful and what was not?
- How can students reflect on their own learning?

Step 6—Set new, high, worthwhile goals. *(Proposition 10)*

- How will you decide when it is time to move on in the lesson sequence?
- What indicators will you use to set new goals?

SSTARS: Here is an acronym to jog your memory.

- **S**tudents: Know your students and how they learn. Proposition 1
- **S**et high, worthwhile, and appropriate goals. Propositions 2 and 3
- **T**each using appropriate, effective strategies. Propositions 3 and 4
- **A**ssess student progress using a variety of evaluation types and forms. Proposition 4
- **R**eflect on your teaching and your students' progress. Proposition 5
- **S**tart the process again.
- See Appendix A for a lesson plan template that uses SSTARS. Revisit the Architecture of Accomplished Teaching found in the General Portfolio Instructions document.

Why It Works! The elements of the Architecture of Accomplished Teaching provide a complete lesson/unit plan that will have the greatest impact on student learning.

What Works! Knowing When to Use the Writing Styles

- Use mainly *descriptive* writing with some analysis for Steps 1, 2, and 3.
- Use mainly *analytical* writing for Step 4.
- Use mainly *analytical and reflective* writing for Steps 5 and 6.

Why It Works!

Use the Architecture of Accomplished Teaching to discern the nuances in the prompt. This will help you use the appropriate writing style for each. The prompts align with the Architecture's steps and using it will help you find evidence of your thinking and teaching to write about.

The Scoring Rubrics and Evaluation of Evidence Guide

The Scoring Rubrics is an underutilized resource that can be a lifesaver. The assessors use them as they score your work. How your component will be scored is not a secret! Everything you need to show evidence of is listed in bullet format in the Scoring Rubrics.

What Works! Including the 3-Cs of Evidence

- *Clear*: Anyone who reads your written commentary should be able to understand what you are saying. You've explained acronyms and educational terms. The sequence of events can be easily followed. Your writing is readable and makes sense.
- *Consistent*: Your writing needs an element of continuity. Don't say one thing in the first paragraph and then contradict it later. Numbers must add up, timelines need to be accurate, and your data shared honestly. Think of threads running through a tapestry.
- *Convincing*: Present the case that you are an accomplished teacher. This means you present your evidence, and it is believable and achievable. The best way to do this is to include specific examples, documentation, rationales, and verification. Including specific examples provides stronger, more convincing evidence. *Examples = Evidence.*

What Works! Studying the Rubrics

- Read all of the levels from Level 4 down to Level 1. You will see a great difference in the quality of evidence described in each one.
- Concentrate on the Level 4 Rubric. Keep it beside you as you write so that you'll know exactly what evidence you need to show. Be sure you have evidence for each bullet. Notice how it aligns with parts of the Architecture of Accomplished Teaching. Also pay attention to presenting specific examples.

- Use the Level 4 Rubric to self-assess each component. Go through it bullet by bullet to be sure you've included everything you need. If something is missing—put it in!

Why It Works!

Using effective tools such as the *Architecture of Accomplished Teaching*, *SSTARS*, and the *Scoring Rubrics* will make the process less frustrating and more meaningful because you'll know where to go for guidance and clarification. Make these tools work for you!

3 Getting Started and Getting Support

Six-Word Memoir: Start sooner—NOW—rather than later!
LYNN, AZ

The Standards, The Lingo, and the Component Requirements

New candidates often don't know where to start. They know they're embarking on a unique journey, but aren't sure what steps to take first. If this describes you, read on.

- Refresh your understanding of the Five Core Propositions. They are the umbrella under which all other National Board documents are organized.
- Read and internalize the NB Standards for your certificate. You must know what they look like in practice and how you use them in your practice.
- Read your *General Portfolio Instructions*. This is an underutilized resource with a wealth of information that is easy to refer to later.
- Study the *Learning Portfolio-Related Terms* (GLOSSARY) section in the General Portfolio Instructions to become familiar with National Board "language" that is specialized and specific to the National Board process. Certain phrases are used repeatedly in your instructions, and the glossary is where they are defined.
- Familiarize yourself with the Component Overviews at the beginning of your Portfolio Instructions to understand the content of each component.

- Study the *What Do I Need to Do?* section of each component for a list of component requirements.

What Works!

Familiarize yourself with the Portfolio Instructions, National Board "language," and structure of the component to give yourself the "big picture" and the tools and confidence to move forward.

Navigating the National Board Website:

The National Board website located at www.nbpts.org contains a wealth of information. Everything you want and need to know to complete Components 3 and 4 is there. But it is a complex site and not always easy to navigate. For the purposes of this chapter, I assume that everyone reading this is already a candidate, so I'll highlight the areas a candidate needs most. Here is a guide to its major components and the documents you'll need to find, download, print, and refer to.

- From the homepage, click on the **For Candidates tab > First Time Candidates.** Now you are on a page with a matrix containing all the National Board documents. Click on the matrix to find:
- All the certificate areas.
- Component Instructions that include the Scoring Rubrics and other Forms you'll submit.
- Certificate Area National Board Standards.
- Documents may be added or revised periodically, so always use the most current resource.
- Recently added features such as ATLAS, a video library of accomplished lessons, and HOMEROOM with many resources, including timelines and much more.

What Works!

These documents become your resources for mapping out your way through the National Board Certification process. Becoming familiar with them will save time and grief!

Why This Works!

Knowing where to go quickly for information is one way to work smart!

Organizing Your National Board Materials:

Once you have a basic overview of the components, it's time to implement some organizational strategies to help keep the myriad of written commentary drafts, paper piles, and artifacts you'll assemble. Here are several systems candidates have used successfully. Pick one or a combination that suits your own style and work habits.

What Works! Organizing KISS Options (Keep It Super Simple!):

- Spiral-bind each set of component instructions. You'll end up with four "books" that are easy to carry as references. They are also sturdy and will stand up to heavy use. Your school may have a machine that does this operation or go to an office supply store.
- Keep instructions in a binder sectioned for each component. On the plus side, this keeps all instructions in one place. But binders can be heavy and awkward to carry, and pages can tear away from the rings. Still, it's a familiar organizational system for many candidates.
- Use a file box with sections or hanging folders for each component and for student work.

Why It Works!

Following a *KISS* system will be a lifesaver. You won't stress over the time you wasted hunting for lost work. Designate a place for your work—and keep it there!

What Works! Organizing Your Written Commentary on Your Computer

- Your computer is your best friend.
- Use a reliable word processing program: Word or Google Docs.
- Follow all instructions regarding font, type size, line spacing, margins, headers, and footers.
- Label each draft with the date. This will assure you are working on the latest version.
- Create a folder for each component and save drafts in their appropriate place.
- Periodically print out drafts or back them up on a flash drive/memory stick that you can use on any computer. This step will save you a lot of stress if your computer crashes or your laptop is lost or stolen. You can also send your work to another computer.
- Remember: save early, save often, and save everything! Back up your files frequently.

Why It Works!

Doing everything you can to keep your writing accessible and safe is prudent and smart. Nothing is worse than losing what you've worked so hard to produce!

What Works! Organize Your Time

Figuring out how to organize your time is by far the most difficult challenge. As you well know, teachers are incredibly busy both at work and at home. Family and work, continually compete for your time and energy. Here are some strategies successful candidates have used to help them cope with the time demands that National Board Certification places on them:

- *Just for this school year*, say no! Eliminate as many committees and school responsibilities as possible. Promise your principal that you'll be back next year.
- *Just for this school year*, say no at home too. Delegate chores and activities. This is not the year to become Team Parent for all of your kids' sports teams and activities. Resign if you already are ... spread the joy and let some other mom or dad take a turn.
- Set aside a designated daily or weekly work/writing period. Some candidates arrange for their spouse to be in charge of the family on a Saturday or Sunday afternoon, or for one weeknight. Other candidates stay late at school once a week or go to their classroom to work on the weekend. This is especially important from January to the deadline date.
- Consider arranging a weekend away from home so you can work undisturbed. Go to a hotel, a cabin, or house-sit for a friend who is away—anywhere you can be alone; OR send your family away!
- In the weeks before the deadline, you'll need additional time to finish and polish components. Plan for it.
- Create a flexible and realistic timeline and do your best to stick to it.

More Strategies

- Avoid procrastination; it will come back to haunt you. Some candidates say they work better under pressure, and that may be true *for a few*. But in the National Board process, you can't quickly dash off a paper and produce a quality portfolio. The portfolio requires a great quantity of quality evidence collected over time, and putting together a successful portfolio is too complex to be done in a hurry.
- Be aware that you will need to work on more than one component at a time if you are tackling more than one component in a year.
- Look at your academic scope and sequence and begin to map out units for your components.
- Look at Component 3 and earmark lessons you teach that will fulfill the requirements.
- Save assessment data to use for Component 4.

Why It Works!

Organizing your time wisely can be a make-or-break factor in the quality of your portfolio submission.

Build a Support System: Cohort Support

When National Board Certification began, candidates were few and far between—both in numbers and location. It wasn't unusual for someone to be the only candidate in their entire state. Fortunately, few candidates face that kind of isolation today. Thanks to National Board Certified Teachers who have certified in the past, a continuum of support has developed across the country. Candidate support systems may be available in or near your school district.

If you are in a cohort, you will work with a Professional Learning Facilitator (PLF) or mentor who will guide your group and be obligated to provide and uphold ethical candidate support according to NBPTS guidelines.

Professional Learning Facilitator's Responsibilities

- Help candidates understand the instructions and process more clearly.
- Help candidates think more clearly and deeply about their teaching practice.
- Help candidates learn to analyze the evidence presented.
- Help candidates engage in self-evaluation.
- Offer patience and encouragement.
- Guide candidates toward making their own decisions about evidence.
- Meet regularly with the candidate cohort and encourage peer collaboration.
- Share knowledge, skills, and experiences.
- Listen nonjudgmentally.
- Ask probing questions.
- Maintain confidentiality.

PLFs cannot:

- Guarantee a certifying score.
- Tell candidates their writing is wrong, flawed, not good enough, or that a component will or will not score well.
- Make a judgment call about portfolio instructions that seem unclear.
- Share NBCT portfolios or videos as teaching examples or tools.
- "Make" candidates into accomplished teachers or a National Board Certified Teacher.
- Create evidence for candidates or tell them how to write the Written Commentary.
- Tell candidates which students to feature, which student work to submit, which videos to submit, or which segment of a video "will work" for sure.
- How to revise, edit, or fix a component.

Candidates' Responsibilities:

If you participate in a cohort, you have responsibilities too ... both to yourself and to the group.

- Make an investment in time and attend scheduled meetings.
- Share fears, concerns, and issues.
- Continually read, review, and apply the Standards.
- Bring work and questions to sessions.
- Keep to established timelines.
- Accept feedback in a professional manner.
- Study the component instructions.
- Come to meetings prepared.
- Maintain confidentiality.
- Commit time to the process.
- Celebrate steps along the way.

What Works!

If you don't have a cohort, you can still find support. Try these ideas:

- Form your own cohort. If there are other candidates in your district or area, organize a monthly meeting. Consider rotating the location so that all candidates host the group.
- Meet with other candidates outside your regular cohort meeting dates.
- Find online support. There are many National Board Facebook pages that offer reliable support:
- National Board Certified Teacher—all certificate areas
- National Board Certified Teacher on Facebook—all certificate areas
- NBCT Support—all certificate areas
- National Board Certification Survival Group—all certificate areas
- National Board Certification for English Teachers
- MCGen National Board Support
- Exceptional Needs—NBCTs and Candidates
- National Board Certification for Worl d Language Teachers
- NBCT Social Studies Support Group
- NBCT Early Adolescent/Adolescent Young Adult Science (EA/AYA)
- National Board Certification—Career and Technical Education (CTE)
- National Board Certification—Early Middle Childhood Literacy (EMC)
- English as a New Language NBCT Candidates

These pages were all active at the time of the writing of this book. There may be other certificate-specific pages—do a search. Some certificate-specific pages may not be as active as the pages for all certification.

Why It Works!

Collaborating with others gives you a sounding board and a place to ask questions and hear others' perspectives. Getting organized with a system that is user-friendly may take some trial and error. Once you find one that works for you, you'll feel more secure moving forward.

4 Component 1, Content Knowledge

A Computer-Based Assessment of Content and Pedagogical Knowledge

Six-Word Memoir: So much to say... so little time!
ROXANNE, OR

Overview: The Purpose of the Component 1 Exercises

Component 1: Content Knowledge is a computer-based assessment requiring candidates to demonstrate knowledge of content and pedagogical practice for their teaching area/subject. Candidates must demonstrate knowledge of developmentally appropriate content, which is necessary for teaching across the full age range and ability levels of the chosen certificate area. Component 1 examines what you know about your content as outlined in the National Board Standards. Component 1 can be completed at any time during your candidacy. Being an accomplished teacher implies mastery of your disciplinary content and pedagogy, so the exercises:

- Focus on knowledge of content and curriculum across the facets of your discipline.
- Focus on themes, ideas, and principles that represent core concepts and curriculum within a discipline.
- Ask you to demonstrate content and pedagogical knowledge with responses to exercises developed and designed by practicing professionals in your certificate area.
- Cover the entire age range of a certificate.

- Allow you to show knowledge of developmentally appropriate content across the full spectrum of your certificate.

Component 1 Instructions Are Your Study Guide

The Component 1 Instructions Document is the only study guide the National Board provides. It explains the types of exercises and contains limited samples. The nature of the exercises and prompts varies among certificates, but all are divided into two types of exercises:

- Selected Response (SR) Items (Multiple Choice)
- Constructed Response (CR) Exercises (Essay-type responses)

Selected Response Items

Selected Response is a fancy term for multiple choice. Each certificate's assessment contains approximately forty-five of this type of item (varies by certificate area). Included in the instructions, found on the Candidate Resource page on the National Board website, are five practice items and an answer key. Most items are scenario-based with four choices. A proven strategy is to narrow your choices to the two most probable answers. You can leave items unanswered, flag them, then go back later to choose.

In the Component 1 document, there is a chart showing the National Board Standards the items are connected to and the percentage of items connected to each Standard. For example, in the Early Childhood Generalist (ECGen) certificate, approximately 30 percent of the forty-five items (13.5 items) connect to the ECGen Standards I and III, 35 percent (15.75) connect to Standards VI and VI, and 35 percent (15.75) connect to Standard IV. Of course, there can't be a fraction of an item, so numbers are approximate. See your Component 1 document for samples in your certificate area. Here are some key features to keep in mind:

- The SR items cover the entire age range of your certificate.
- You are expected to demonstrate knowledge of developmentally appropriate content and pedagogy across the full range of your certificate.

- In most certificates, the items cover both content and pedagogy. Middle school and high school certificates tend to focus more on content than pedagogy. The Math Certificate's Component 1 is mostly content.

Certificate-Specific Pathways

Several certificates offer specialized "Pathways" connected to the Constructed Responses. Candidates choose the path that best represents the greater part of their teaching. The Selected Response items cover overall, general knowledge of the subject area; the Constructed Response section allows candidates to use their main teaching context as the basis for their responses. Information regarding these pathways is found in the *Choosing the Right Certificate* document found on the Candidate Resources page on the National Board website. Candidates choose the path when registering for the Component 1 Assessment. Here are examples of certificates which offer the paths. Again, read your C1 instructions carefully.

Career and Technical Education	English as New Language
Exceptional Needs Specialist	Music
AYA Science	EA/YA World Languages

Constructed Response Items

These are the "essay question" parts of the assessment. In this section, you will construct responses to three exercises, each representing a scenario that could occur within a teaching context, or in the case of the Math certificate, to solve problems. All exercises in all certificates follow the same structure.

- **Introduction:** A brief description of the exercise.
- **Criteria for Scoring:** The Level 4 Rubric that assessors use to evaluate your response.
- **Directions:** How to use the computer to view the exercise.
- **Stimulus:** The actual scenario and/or resource used as the basis for your response. Not all certificate areas contain a stimulus.

Certificate-Specific Examples:

EC/MCGeneralist; EC/MC Literacy: Reading/Language Arts; EC/YA Exceptional Needs Specialist. These certificates link content to pedagogy. Knowing how to teach the concept is the content. Exercises may ask candidates to:

- Analyze student responses to a stimulus/topic.
- Analyze, identify, and interpret student misconceptions/errors about a topic.
- Describe thorough, detailed, and appropriate instructional strategies and materials to correct misconceptions and/or extend understanding of the topic.
- Plan worthwhile goals and a developmentally appropriate instructional sequence based on the Architecture of Accomplished Teaching (AAT) that will accomplish the goals.
- Provide a thorough, detailed rationale to justify decisions that fit these students, at this time, in this setting.
- ENS candidates choose a specialty "path" (done at C1 registration) for the Constructed Responses.

Science, Math, Social Studies/History, CTE

These certificates may have exercises that emphasize connections between specialty areas and another context within the discipline, as well as your breadth of knowledge across disciplines. Pedagogy is less important than the depth and breadth of content knowledge.

- Some certificates choose a specialty "path" that follows their area of specialization. Check your instructions.
- Math exercises are mostly problem-solving in the areas of algebra, calculus, discrete mathematics, geometry, statistics, and data analysis.
- Social Studies/History certificate asks you to demonstrate the breadth of your knowledge using graphics and documents in the areas of US History, World History, Political Science, Economics, and Geography.

These are a few examples to illustrate the nature of the exercises/prompts found in the various certificate areas. Your Component 1 Instruction document contains information about the exercise topics for your certificate. Analyzing examples is crucial for your preparation.

How to Study for Component 1:

- Start by reading the C1 instructions in their entirety. They contain a wealth of information to help you understand the exercises. The samples and practice exercises provide the starting point.
- Make a "nutshell" for each conatructed response exercise. This will break the prompts into bite-sized chunks that make it easier to grasp what is asked in each exercise. Create a chart or matrix for each exercise. Make a column for each part of the exercises: Introduction, Criteria for Scoring, and so on, and add a column listing the verbs used in the explanation and scoring rubric. Analyze the following chart of exercises from three thesecertificate areas (Table 4.1):

WHAT WORKS! Create Your Own Sample Exercises:

- Find a certificate-like group/cohort and work together to create new exercises. You may find help with this on National Board Facebook pages or within your own local cohort.
- Use AI to generate similarly worded exercises on a different topic. Type a question related to a prompt you have, such as this (AYA Science) example: *In 500 words or less, describe 3 historical scientific events or discoveries, explain how another science discipline is related to the event/discovery and now that event/discovery has affected society.*
- **Read the National Board *Use of AI* Rules found on page 10 in the General Portfolio Instructions.**

Internet, Books, and Other Resources:

- GOOGLE is your friend! Use key words in your Component 1 Instructions.
- ECGen search for Play.
- Physical Education looks for Exercise Science.
- SS/History looks for Important American Documents.
- EMC Literacy looks for Reading Miscues.

Table 4.1 Constructed Response Analysis

ECGEN	VERBS	STIMULUS	TEACHER ACTION
Show your ability to analyze, infer, make inferences about a student's reading development. Identify strengths strategies based on strengths. Include resources and a rationale for your choices.	Analyze	1 Student progress report	Identify 2 strengths.
	Infer		Identify 1 goal.
	Identify		Choose strategy/activity to reach goal.
	Plan		Resources/materials
	Include		Rationales
	Provide		
MCGEN			
Identify math misconception/error.	Identify	Student Work	Identify error pattern in problem.
Identify concepts/skills needed for understanding & provide strategies with rationale to assist understanding of the skill/concept.	Provide		Identify concepts needed to correct error.
			Provide strategies to correct error.
			Provide rationale for choices.
EMC LITERACY : Reading/LA			
Analyze a student writing sample	Analyze	Writing Sample	Find 1 weakness
Describe developmental characteristics & propose two strategies to address weakness or build on strengths.	Describe		Find 1 strength
			Describe developmental level in detail.
			Provide 2 appropriate strategies

(*Continued*)

Table 4.1 (Continued)

ECGEN	VERBS	STIMULUS	TEACHER ACTION
AYA/ELA			
Use your knowledge of ELA to analyze one student's response to a text & discuss strategies the student could use to correct a misconception in the reading.	Analyze	Reading Passage	Identify 1 misconception
	Identify	Student Response	Identify & describe 2 strategies to address the misconception.
	Describe		Provide a rationale for each strategy.
AYA:SCIENCE			
Use your knowledge of science to describe a scientific event or discovery & discuss the scientific knowledge needed to understand the event/discovery. Explain how another science discipline is related to the event/discovery & describe how the event/discovery has affected society. has affected society.	Analyze	Scenario	Discuss the event or discovery.
	Discuss		Discuss the scientific knowledge needed to understand the event or discovery.
	Explain		Explain how a science discipline other than science is related to the related to the event/discovery.
			Discuss 2 effects the event or discovery has had on society. has had on society.

Component 1 Instruction Document

- Your State Standards provide a rich resource for finding topics for the age levels in your certificates. Make lists of possible topics. For example, topics that might fit an MCGen science exercise include Life Cycles, Energy, Earth and Space, Motion and Forces, Climate and Weather, Properties of Matter, the Solar System, and Body Systems. A Social Studies/History candidate might investigate Government,

Economics, Early Civilizations, Regions and Places, Human Systems, Population Migration, and Exploration.
- Book Series such as *Everything You Need to Know about Science* or *What Every Sixth Grader Should Know*.
- Academic Testing Resources such as Praxis, Advanced Placement materials, and College Board Exam Study Guides.
- Internet Resources, including

Quizlet	Kahn Academy	Mystery Science	YouTube
Crash Course	ourdocuments.com	NBSS Standards	
100 Greatest Documents in American History			

Why These Work!

Using a variety of resources will broaden your understanding of the C1 items and content—all the better to prepare you to do your best.

What You'll Find at the Testing Center

Besides your Component 1 Instructions, the next most important document is the *Component 1: Content Knowledge, Assessment Center Policy and Guidelines* document. It contains all you need to know about preparing for, arriving at, and testing at the Assessment Center. Security is tight at all centers, so be prepared. This document will tell you all you need to know about appointments, allowed "comfort aids," and much more. Here are some highlights:

- Most certificate areas receive a whiteboard and dry-erase marker for making notes, and so on.
- Math and Science specialty areas receive an *online* scientific calculator.
- Music and Math candidates receive a response booklet and a pencil.

Pearson VUE Website

An extremely valuable tutorial is available on the Pearson website at pearsonvue.com. There is a live link on page 10 of the *Component 1: Content Knowledge* document. EVERYONE should take the tutorial to familiarize yourself with the format of the assessment screens.

Writing for Component 1:

The writing styles you used for the various Written Commentaries provide the foundation to address the prompts in the Constructed Response exercises. You still want to use focused, to-the-point sentences. However, there are no space limits—the only limitation is time—so you can choose the format that works best for you: paragraph form or bullet form. Choose a format that supports your thinking and organizational style. You can mix the two formats as well.

What Works! Component 1: Writing Strategies for Success

- Use the whiteboard you're given to jot down notes BEFORE the testing times begin. This allows quick references in order to use time wisely.
- If you get stumped, jog your thinking by starting your response with a sentence stem that restates the question.
- Use bullets if it helps organize your thinking. Assessors are fine with a bullet format, and you have all the space you want.
- Match your responses to the prompt. If a prompt asks for *two* strategies—give *two*—no more, no less. There are no bonus points awarded for more—and it uses up time.
- Emphasize National Board Standards, the impact on student learning, and real-world application.
- Skip introductions and conclusions. There is no scoreable evidence in either, and they eat up valuable time writing.
- Use facts and statistical details you know to be true, then back them up with evidence (examples).

- Cite specific examples. Illustrated evidence is strong evidence.
- Formulate and utilize cause-and-effect information where appropriate. This exemplifies higher reasoning skills.
- Be firm in your opinions. Avoid "I think . . . " or "It may be possible to . . . " Such phrases weaken the discussion.
- Include rationales. Rationales are powerful analyses. Many exercises ask directly for them. Put them in anywhere you can.
- Respond to every part of every prompt. Omitting information earns no points.

Why These Work!

Knowing what to expect, how to study and prepare, and how to write responses will lower your anxiety and boost your confidence. You'll do better if you feel ready.

What Works! More Strategies for Success with Component 1

- Study! Refresh your knowledge with current information in your content area. Brush up on weak areas and solidify your strengths.
- Keep some lessons you've taught that worked well in mind and use them as the basis for your brainstorming. You don't have to completely reinvent the wheel.
- If your test includes reading, explore different themes in literature used within the age range of your certificate area, and specify titles that illustrate those themes.
- Check your state's subject and grade level-specific Standards to generate lists of possible topics.
- Research National Standards in your subject area.
- Use your colleagues as a resource to discuss strategies. For example, generalists might talk with colleagues who teach younger/older students regarding reading strategies such as miscue analysis and running records. Middle school/high school candidates might talk with an interventionist or resource teacher for ideas.

- Have some ideas in mind for differentiating lessons to show how you can plan for different abilities and styles of learning.
- High school and middle school teachers may benefit from studying PRAXIS and Advanced Placement study guides.
- Know the steps of the Architecture of Accomplished Teaching (AAT) and be able to apply them to any lesson an exercise asks you to "plan."
- Read the *whole* exercise. There are usually several parts, each requiring a response.
- Analyze the directions, paying special attention to the verbs. Focus on these areas:
- *Content*: reading, math, science, social studies, and so on.
- *Prompt Format*: a scenario, a stimulus piece, a document, a graphic, a problem
- *Action Words:* identify, explain, discuss, describe, plan, provide
- *The Task:* Show knowledge of, Analyze student errors, give examples of
- Make up your own prompts. Try designing prompts for various age groups within your certificate area.
- Practice with another candidate.
- Practice with a timer. Set a timer for thirty minutes, then write, write, write! You will get faster each time.
- Budget your time. You get thirty minutes total for each Constructed Response. If that exercise has three parts, you should aim to spend about ten minutes on each part.
- Have confidence in your own experience and knowledge.
- Answer each part completely before moving on. Address all parts of each prompt. Once you leave an exercise, you cannot return to it.
- Use the Level 4 Rubric, which is shown within the exercise, as a touchstone for each exercise.

What Works! Even More Tips for Component 1 Success

Try to schedule your assessment after you've submitted other components to give yourself a break and some time to prepare.

- Choose and confirm a date as quickly as possible after the Testing Window opens. This will give you the widest choice of dates and times. Avoid scheduling your date on the last day tests can be scheduled. If "life" happens, and a postponement is necessary, this can be complicated.
- Read all the Assessment Center documents so you'll know exactly what you can and cannot take. The centers have very strict requirements.
- Make sure you have a *current* state-issued ID with a photo on it that you can show.
- Dress in layers; the centers can be hot or cold.
- Take the ten-minute break offered between sections.
- Take a test drive to your center in advance of your appointment. Take the drive during the time you'll actually be driving there. This will give you peace of mind.
- Plan to arrive at least thirty minutes early.
- Take the Pearson Vue tutorial offered before going to the testing center. It will familiarize you with the format and layout of the screen. Especially practice scrolling, as each exercise contains several prompts and you may need to scroll down to see all the parts. The tutorial and a link are found in the *Component 1: Content Knowledge Assessment Center Policy and Guidelines* document found on the National Board Website on the Candidate Resources page.

Why These Work!

With purposeful planning, you can approach the Assessment Center and Component 1 with confidence. Use what you already know about accomplished teaching practices to show what you know about your subject-specific content.

5 Component 2, Differentiation in Instruction

Sharing Accomplished Teaching through Student Work Samples

Overview

In all certificate areas, Component 2 centers on differentiation as shown through the analysis of student work samples. You collect student work samples from a series of lessons, then describe, analyze, and reflect on the work of one or more students to show growth over time. The work samples are the evidence of the effectiveness of your planning and teaching, your understanding of the Architecture of Accomplished Teaching (AAT), and your ability to describe, analyze, and reflect on your teaching practice. Work samples can take many forms, depending on the certificate area. Samples can be pencil/paper samples, projects, objects, or, for music candidates, the "sample" is a video.

Currently, in most districts, student achievement is measured primarily through standardized test data. The National Board cares about student achievement but recognizes a variety of ways learning can be demonstrated. In Component 2, your analysis of student work is important not only because of the scores it produces but also because it is the way assessors will evaluate the effectiveness of your teaching practice. When grading, you look for evidence in student work that shows understanding of the content or skill taught. But NB assessors go deeper and look at your *analysis* and *reflection* of the student work to see what evidence of effective teaching it provides.

The measure of accomplished teaching is its capacity to impact student learning. Effective teaching means that as a result of your teaching practices, student achievement improves. This is why you plan engaging, appropriate lessons *for these students, at this time, in this setting*. This is why you'll choose the student work you'll feature very carefully. The focus of Component 2 is on your teaching, not on student achievement, but if you choose to feature a student who did not show growth—or as much as you'd hoped—be prepared to explain why and what your next steps will be.

What Do You Need To Do?

Each certificate area has different requirements, but all certificates ask you to:

- Show your ability to evaluate learning strengths and needs for individual students.
- Plan and implement appropriate differentiated instruction for those students.
- Analyze and modify instructional strategies and materials based on ongoing monitoring and assessment.
- Choose students to feature. Your instructions tell you how many you'll feature. Exceptional needs specialists and literacy candidates choose one student; most other certificates choose two students.
- If choosing more than one, choose students with different needs either in their abilities, learning styles, performance, interests, and/or other characteristics. This will allow you to show how you differentiate your instruction to meet their needs.
- Select work samples that demonstrate your approach to teaching and that exemplify each student's needs.

Read your certificate's Component 2 instructions carefully because each certificate has requirements specific to that subject area. Most certificates focus on writing samples within a discipline, but instructions vary greatly from certificate to certificate. For example, an MCGen submits samples of expository and narrative writing, while Science and Math candidates choose assignments connected to a major scientific or mathematical idea and activities they select. Because Music is a performance subject, Music candidates submit student work samples in the form of videos rather than pencil-and-paper assignments. Each certificate has different requirements and it's your job to know what you're required to submit in your certificate.

Unpacking the Prompts:

Understanding the language and intent of the prompts can be challenging. On the surface, it can feel as if you're answering the same thing multiple times. Each prompt is written to elicit evidence of the Five Core Propositions and the NB Standards in your teaching practice, and to reference the steps in the Architecture of Accomplished Teaching (AAT)—the helix graphic found in the General Portfolio Instructions. The AAT is the National Board version of an accomplished lesson/unit plan.

Notice the directions in the Written Commentary ask you to *address* the prompts, not *answer* them. This is more than just a nuance of wording. *Address* means to write what is true for you, in your teaching context. *Answer* implies something more right/wrong, more concrete. The prompts are designed to elicit open-ended responses that fit your teaching situation. They don't dictate any particular teaching style, and most likely your responses won't sound like anyone else's because you are describing only your practice, not your colleague's down the hall.

What Works!

- Take the prompts apart and analyze what they ask for. Pay attention to the *verbs* because they tell you what you must *do*.
- Look for *key words*. EXAMPLE: *Relevant* is used in multiple prompts in the Instructional Context. Look up *relevant* in a thesaurus and make note of the many synonyms. Which fits what you want to say? Do this with other key words as well—even if you think you know the meaning. Sometimes a synonym "clicks" in our brain and enhances understanding.
- If prompts sound alike, analyze them further. There is always something that distinguishes one from another. Sometimes one builds upon a previous prompt and takes it deeper. Or, in some certificates, similar prompts elicit responses about a student in different areas of the curriculum. For example, the ELA certificates ask

the same questions about students in both the reading and writing domains. Same question; different responses.

- Notice that prompts are connected to various steps in the AAT. A prompt that asks about setting goals would be connected to Step 2. A prompt asking about resources would connect to Step 3. Prompts asking about evaluating connect to Step 4, prompts about next steps connect to Step 5, and Step 6 starts the cycle over again. FYI: Step 1 is ALWAYS about knowledge of students. See the AAT Graphic and SSTARS Lesson Plan in the Appendix.
- Address all parts of a prompt. Many have multiple parts. Pay attention to commas, semicolons, and colons that separate parts. Your Component 2 Instructional Context section has this prompt, or one very similar:

What are the relevant characteristics of this class that influenced your instructional strategies for this theme or topic of concern: ethnic, cultural, and linguistic diversity; the range of abilities of the students; and the personality of the class?

This prompt asks for information about five characteristics, and you must address each one, succinctly and clearly: ethnic, cultural, linguistic diversity, range of abilities, and personality of the class. Write about all of them. Don't leave any of them out.

Planning Lessons Using the Architecture of Accomplished Teaching and SSTARS:

The Architecture of Accomplished Teaching (AAT) is the National Board version of an accomplished lesson/unit plan. The National Board has created a graphic consisting of a tightly woven helix showing the steps an accomplished lesson/unit contains. The AAT is shown in the Appendix pages. The helix is read from the bottom up. Each step is connected to one or more of the Five Core Propositions and one or more National Board Standards. I've simplified the steps into an acronym called SSTARS. Here are the SSTARS steps:

- Step 1: Students—Knowledge of Students.
- Step 2: Set Goals.
- Step 3: Teach the content matched to the goals.
- Step 4: Assess learning of the goals.

- Step 5: Reflect on student learning.
- Step 6: Start over again. Use assessment data and reflection to set new goals.

Planning Backwards: Plan with the End in Mind:

Don't put yourself in the position of teaching lessons, then crossing your fingers hoping the evidence the assessors expect to see will be "in there." That is not the smartest plan! Your goal is to satisfy the Level 4 Scoring Rubric, and *planning backwards* is an effective strategy to meet that goal. By *planning backwards*, I mean to design your lesson sequence to fit the requirements of the component rather than trying to make the component fit the lessons you taught. Like when planning a trip, you must have the destination in mind before you start in order to get there, pack the right gear, and so on. Reaching the destination is super important. Plan lessons that embed the evidence assessors expect to see. This is smart planning—not cheating!

What Works!

Start with the evidence assessors expect to see. How do you know what that is? Their expectations are laid out in the Level 4 Rubric. Every certificate and every component has a Rubric statement that references goals.

- Here is one from the ELA Level 4 Rubric: . . . *the teacher has a thorough knowledge of students as individual learners and sets high, worthwhile, and attainable goals for growth.*
- The corresponding rubric statement from the Science certificate is: . . . *the teacher is able to select and justify a major idea in science and related learning goals as appropriate for his or her students and specific teaching context.*
- In the ECGen certificate, the rubric statement reads that *the teacher sets high, worthwhile, and appropriate goals and objectives for children's learning that are tightly connected to instruction.*

Whatever your certificate, your writing needs to show examples that you have met this criteria with your students. Here is a fabricated example of a poorly designed lesson plan that would NOT meet the Level 4 Rubric goal statement:

- The goals of a science lesson for kindergarten students are to learn the stages in the life cycle of pumpkins and be able to draw the pumpkin in it's various life-cycle stages (seed, sprout, vine, flower, green pumpkin, mature pumpkin etc.).
- The lesson plan: Students will read Halloween and "fall" books about pumpkins and write stories with pumpkin illustrations. The teacher will set up centers where students can see inside a cut pumpkin, count the seeds, taste foods made with pumpkin, and draw jack-o-lantern faces onto paper pumpkins. Sounds fun, right?
- Question: Why will this lesson NOT meet the Level 4 rubric?
- Answer: None of the activities planned support the teacher's goal of learning the stages of a pumpkin's life cycle. None of the centers' activities focus on the life cycle of a pumpkin, the goals and the instruction don't match. They are not connected.

More Tips:

- Highlight the words *clear, consistent, and convincing* in the heading of the your Level 4 Rubric. *Clear* means anyone can understand what you've written. *Consistent* means important concepts and evidence are connected and might be discussed in more than one place and/or in more than one way. *Convincing* means you've provided evidence (examples) to back up your statements.
- Read the bulleted Level 4 Rubric list. These items are the evidence you need in the lessons to demonstrate in your teaching practice. Paraphrase and create your own list in your own words. I've heard of candidates putting the statements into an AI program and asking it to rephrase the statement for clarity if the meaning isn't clear to you.
- Include evidence (examples) of each bullet in your lessons and show in the Written Commentary how they are connected to your teaching and the student work.

The way to show *clear, consistent, and convincing* evidence to the assessors is to use student work samples to point out specific examples/features and explain exactly what you did and why. The assessors have only your Written Commentary and the student work you submit to use as evaluation. These are the only evidence assessors have that informs them about your practice. The work samples do not receive a separate score, rather they provide support for what you say in the Written Commentary. They are part of the holistic scoring process. They are the *evidence* that backs up what you write and what you claim.

Use the Level 4 Rubric to Plan and Evaluate

What might it look like to incorporate the Level 4 Rubric evidence into the planning of your lessons? To illustrate a teacher's thinking and planning process, using the MCGen Rubric as an example, read the *hypothetical notes* a teacher might write when planning writing experiences using the Level 4 Rubric Statement.

The MCGen Level 4 Rubric Example:

In the Component 2 rubric in the MCGen certificate, there are seven bullets, all of which connect to one or more of the Five Core Propositions and NB Standards.

The Teacher's Thinking/Planning Brainstorming Process:

- "I'll pre-assess to determine where my students are in the writing process."
- I'll plan differentiated writing experiences over a period of time that address the learning differences represented by my students.
- I'll plan narrative and expository prompts that my students will find interesting and engaging and that will provide outlets for them to communicate ideas with a variety of audiences.
- I'll provide reference and vocabulary materials for my new English speakers.
- I'll provide choices to meet my students' various learning styles, knowledge levels, and interests.
- I'll analyze students' work and provide specific feedback to students so they will know their strengths and where they can improve.
- I'll post assessments to evaluate students' learning of the goals and to inform my planning and instruction of next steps.
- I'll reflect on the lessons in order to make meaningful changes in future teaching.

These "thinking statements" address every bullet in the Level 4 Rubric. If a teacher puts this thinking into action, and writes well about the experiences, the Level 4 Rubric will have been addressed. You can see how much of the teaching process is embedded in the notes and how directly they reference the AAT. You want your Written Commentary to reveal the thinking that goes into planning and teaching the lesson. This is what provides strong evidence of the rubric.

First person is the strongest "voice" to use when explaining your teaching. It's uncomfortable for many to talk about themselves, but in this case, it isn't bragging. It's necessary in order to explain what you do and what you think. A strong, first-person voice adds value to your writing.

Making Your Selections:

Every certificate has important selections to make. These include

- the assignments/activities students will do to produce the work samples
- the student or students you will feature
- the topic(s) and lesson sequence to teach that address the C2 requirements to use differentiation to address diverse needs

What Works! Seven Ways to Differentiate Instruction:

- Content: Differentiate the content students learn or the ways students access the information.
- Process: How students take in and make sense of the content.
- Product: How students show what they know, understand, and can do.
- Environment: The climate, tone, and/or arrangement of the space address students' needs.
- Readiness: How prepared a student is (background knowledge, experiences, etc.) to reach a goal.
- Interests: Patterns, affinities, curiosities that motivate learning.
- Learning Styles: A student's preferred approaches to learning.

These strategies work whether addressing differentiation for one or two students or a class.

What Works! Choose the Student(s) and Work Samples to Feature:

- Choose more students than the number required in case someone moves away or someone's work doesn't quite pan out the way you'd hoped.
- Choose students (or a student) *for whom there is something to say*. Select students for whom your teaching has clearly, consistently, and convincingly made a difference. Choosing wisely gives you the opportunity to showcase your knowledge of students, content, and pedagogy. Choosing the highest or lowest achieving students in a class may not be the best strategy for this work.
- Select students through whom you can clearly, consistently, and convincingly show the range of your teaching toolbox. This means you can use multiple strategies to reach students with varying needs.
- Choose students who show different needs in ability, learning style, interests, and/or performance. This gives the opportunity to show how you can differentiate to meet those needs.
- Select students whose work allows you to show the effectiveness of your teaching through differentiation.
- Choose work samples that demonstrate the effectiveness of your teaching strategies.
- Choose tasks/assignments worthy of your students' time and effort—not just busy work.
- Choose samples that align with and support the goals and objectives stated for the lessons. Remember the pumpkin lesson example from earlier where the students' work did not support the stated goals.
- Choose samples that show students improving their performance over time.
- Choose assignments that challenge students' thinking and show learning across disciplines. Even work samples from very young children can do this. For Component 2, toss the worksheets.
- Choose assignments that feature open-ended questions or prompts—even with young students. These are stronger choices because they provide more opportunity for creativity, critical thinking, and showing understanding. Most worksheets don't do that.

- Choose samples that allow students to demonstrate a range of understanding (think Bloom's Taxonomy) of the content.
- Choose samples that show progression through a topic and progress over time. Some certificates ask you to choose activities that "build on each other" for this very reason.
- Choose samples for which you can give meaningful feedback, beyond *good job* or *great*. Feedback should be specific guidance which will help the student know how to improve next time. EXAMPLE: *You used commas correctly in this writing!* or *Remember to use commas with words in a series.*

Why These Work!

Making careful selections allows you to showcase your differentiation strategies and the depth and breadth of your teaching practice.

What Works! Save (Almost) Everything:

Save more than you think you'll need. Save samples connected to the goals you set for the lesson sequences. Here is a list of items to save:

- Evaluation rubrics—ones you make, ones students make, ones from your curriculum. These can be strong evidence of self-assessment, student engagement, and learning.
- Class sets of work or copies. This will give you a wide selection to choose from. Date all work.
- A variety of *types* of work that connect to your lesson sequence. Depending on the certificate area, examples might include research reports, opinion pieces, journal writing, and claim/evidence writing.
- Save work from more than the required number of students. This will give you choices and might save you if someone you planned to feature moves away.
- Take photos of work samples that are too large or three-dimensional (projects) to scan.

Why These Work!

Such examples showcase your thinking, strategies, and accomplished teaching.

Instructional Materials:

The NB definition of instructional materials is found in the General Portfolio Instructions, in the Portfolio-Related Terms section. An instructional material is an item used or produced during a teaching sequence. Assessors review the materials to better understand the activity featured in your video recording (music) or Written Commentary. Instructional materials can run the gamut from a rubric, to an Internet Web page, to curriculum materials, graphic organizers, charts, manipulatives, and almost anything else you use to teach a lesson.

Analyzing Student Work:

Planning and teaching the lessons that produce the work samples show evidence of four of the Five Core Propositions and the National Board Standards. They show evidence of:

- Your knowledge of your students (Proposition 1)
- Your knowledge of your content area (Proposition 2)
- Thinking systematically about your practice (Proposition 3)
- Your ability to manage and monitor your students' learning (Proposition 4)

Analyzing student work for National Board submission is very different from the typical quick, day-to-day grading teachers often do. Such grading might entail assigning a mark, score, or symbol such as a smiley face or star before returning the paper to the student and going on to the next topic. Grading papers isn't analysis to the depth the National Board expects candidates to probe. Think of analysis as *insight*—what *you see* in a student's work. Analyzing means looking at student work in order to understand and improve it.

- Notice how students, *how* they understand the learning goal(s).
- Notice which *skills* the student already knows.
- Notice *misconceptions* about the learning goal.

- Notice the *mistakes* the student makes.
- Notice *indicators* that the assignment/activity was successful—or not.
- Decide *what the student needs next* to move closer to learning the goal.

Evidence = Examples

When you look for evidence to write about, you are looking for examples in the student work samples. You are like a lawyer laying out a case. You make a claim about the work, then use the examples from the sample as your evidence to support that the claim is true.

What Works!

- Be specific when analyzing and writing about student work. *When Ian wrote ___, this showed me ___.*
- Add specifics to your writing. This is how assessors evaluate your level of knowledge. For example, saying a student *can't write* really doesn't say much at all. Instead, show you know why the student struggles with writing. For example:
- The students' thoughts are disorganized.
- The student omits vowels when spelling.
- The student doesn't show a beginning, middle, or end of a story.
- The student doesn't give reasons for an opinion.
- The student doesn't include details/specifics.
- The student makes claims without evidence.

After you analyze for specificity, plan your instruction to include what the student needs next to improve (graphic organizers, spelling dictionary, lists, a thesaurus, etc.). This demonstrates your knowledge of your subject area, how to teach it, your National Board Standards, and is evidence you've addressed step 6 on the AAT

Why This Works!

The kind of analysis teachers do every day connects to strong evidence of what accomplished teachers should know and be able to do. You already know how to do this!

Composing the Written Commentary:

Imagine you've planned and taught lessons about an important topic for Component 2. You've collected stacks of work samples that support the goals and objectives, and represent the activities and assessments you planned. You've chosen the students for whom there is something to say, and their samples, your notes, and the Level 4 Rubric are beside you at the computer. You are ready to tackle the prompts. You are ready to start writing. But start where? Write what?

What Works!

- Respond to each prompt with information that is true for you and the featured students.
- Discuss your analysis of the work and cite specific examples that led you to these conclusions.
- Break the prompts into parts, paying particular attention to the verbs, such as describe, cite, or explain that shows what you do or what the student does.
- Pay attention to the *nouns* in the prompts—especially whether they are singular or plural, and whether they refer to the class or the featured student(s).

The Instructional Context:

The *Instructional Context* section of Component 2 is the largest descriptive passage you will write in Component 2. This section gives assessors a sense of your teaching context (situation) and the featured class and student(s). Tell enough to give the assessors a realistic picture of the characteristics that shape your teaching and the personality of the class. Be sure to respond to every part of each prompt, but keep as close to page suggestion as possible (one page in most certificates, two pages in some certificates) because you'll need space later for other, more evidence-rich sections of the components. Here are some *partial, hypothetical* descriptive passages that might be found in a Component 2 Instructional Context:

- *EA/Science*: The featured class consists of twenty-seven students, who are 11–14 years old. Science is the first period of the day. Several students are habitually tardy, which makes it difficult to begin instruction on time. Seven students are English language learners who leave ten minutes early to go to the Resource Room for language instruction. Therefore, I must complete the essential lesson elements before they go.
- *MCGeneralist*: Jenny is young and immature for a fourth grader. She reads at a second grade level and struggles putting her thoughts on paper. She often misspells words and writes entire stories without any punctuation. She likes to work with a partner but has difficulty staying focused on the task.
- *AYA/Math*: All students in this AP Statistics class plan to attend a four-year college. All students have passed Algebra 2, and some are currently enrolled in Calculus 3. Nearly half of the students have taken an AP course, but none have taken any statistics courses prior to this class.
- *EA/YA/Career and Technical Education*: The majority of learners in this computer class are in the "Basic" reading category which is below grade level. Four students are "Below Basic" which signifies they are far below grade level. Only one student in the whole class is "Proficient" and on grade level. The class personality is pleasant and cooperative, and most students are generally on-task.

Description Writing:

- Be succinct. Say enough to paint the picture, then stop.
- Decide which facts and details are significant and emphasize those.
- Concentrate on facts and details that show an impact on teaching or learning.

- Resist the urge to tell *everything*. Details matter, but don't go on and on.
- Description should be the smallest portion of your writing outside the Instructional Context section.
- Follow suggested page limits. They are there for a reason—to keep you from writing too much description and not enough analysis and reflection.
- Support the description with details and specific examples—but not too many.

Electronic Submission at a Glance:

This chart, found after the Written Commentary prompts, can be a valuable resource when submission day comes. It lists every item that must be submitted. It details the format each part should be in, the number of files, the length of each file, and additional information. This is your checklist of all the requirements. Use it! It takes the mystery out of what needs to be submitted.

Why These Work!

Component 2 is about examining how you differentiate your teaching practice through the lens of student work samples. Analyzing student work is among the most important things teachers do because it can have such a significant impact on student learning and should have an impact on planning next steps. You're already experienced with this skill, but may not have had to analyze and reflect on it in written form until now. Writing clearly, consistently, and convincingly showcases your accomplished teaching. This component is an opportunity to let your expertise shine through.

6 Writing for the National Board

Six-Word Memoir: Read, write, reflect, revise, repeat . . . submit!
NANETTE, AZ

Present Your Case

Writing National Board entries is unlike any other kind of writing you've done. It's not like the creative writing assignments you did in high school or college. It's not even like writing a term paper or Master's thesis. Your score isn't determined by your grammar or sentence structure, fancy language, or the number of research citations you include. In fact, some attributes of what is typically considered "good writing" don't necessarily apply here. So, what is it like?

Writing for the National Board is, above all else, *evidentiary*, meaning written to present *evidence*. Your sole purpose is to present evidence of your accomplished teaching, learning, leadership, and collaboration. It isn't quite as easy as pie, but it isn't rocket science either. You must make a case for your accomplished teaching the same way a lawyer argues a case in the courtroom—by presenting strong *evidence*. You are the defendant acting as your own attorney, presenting evidence of what you do in your classroom. Your student work samples, videos, and responses to the prompts are the evidence of your accomplished teaching. The assessor is the judge and jury.

Overview of the Three Styles of Writing: Description, Analysis, and Reflection

Just as an attorney uses questioning styles to elicit evidence, the National Board uses writing styles that can be explained in three verbs: *describe*, *analyze*, and *reflect*. Each prompt connects to one or more writing styles to help you present information that is *clear, consistent*, and *convincing*. *Describe*, *analyze*, and *reflect* are verbs that tell what you must *do*. The noun forms, *description, analysis*, and *reflection*, are the *results* of your actions.

Description Tells What

When you describe something, you tell *about* it; you tell *what* occurred. In court, a witness gives the facts in order to paint a clear picture of a situation. There should be no interpretation or judgment in descriptive writing. In a National Board entry, you respond with enough information for the assessor to form a picture or impression of what you want to depict. Key words in prompts that ask for description include

- Tell
- Explain
- List
- Describe
- What...?

A descriptive passage:

- Tells or retells the main facts.
- Is logically ordered.
- Has enough detail to set the scene and give assessors a basic sense of the class, student, or situation you need to describe.
- Contains accurate, precise enumeration where appropriate.
- Includes elements and features that allow an assessor to "see what you see."
- May be used in conjunction with analysis. You often need to describe the subject or situation you are analyzing so that it is visible to the assessor, making the analysis more meaningful. But the borders between them can be fuzzy.

Description in the Writing:

Description is the easiest type of writing to do. Most teachers find description easy to write and typically tend to describe way too much. Although it is important to use description to give the facts and paint a picture of your class, students, and activities, it isn't the most important type of writing. Why? *It is the least evidentiary of the writing styles.* Description sets the tone, draws a picture, and gives the facts. But it doesn't deliver much, if any, evidence. That is the task of analysis and reflection. Keep description at a minimum.

The *Instructional Context* section of Component 2, and any of the *Context Forms*, is the largest descriptive passages you will write. These give assessors a sense of your teaching context and the featured class and student(s). Tell enough to give the assessors a realistic picture of the characteristics that shape your teaching and the personality of the class. Be sure to respond to *every part* of each prompt, but keep as close to page suggestion as possible (one page in most certificates, two pages in some) because you'll need space later for other, more evidence-rich sections of the entries. Here are some *hypothetical* descriptive passages that might be found in an Instructional Context:

- *EA/Science*: The featured class consists of twenty-seven students, who are 11–14 years old. Science is the first period of the day, and several students are habitually tardy, which makes it difficult to begin instruction on time. Seven students are English language learners who leave ten minutes early to go to the Resource Room for language instruction. Therefore I must complete the essential lesson elements before they go.
- *MC/Generalist*: Jenny is both young and immature for a fourth grader. She reads at a second grade level and has particular trouble putting her thoughts on paper. She often misspells words and writes entire stories without using any punctuation. She likes to work with a partner but has difficulty staying focused on the task.
- *AYA/Math*: All students in this AP Statistics class plan to attend a four-year college. All students in the class have passed Algebra 2, and some are currently enrolled in Calculus 3. Nearly half of the students have taken an AP course before, but none have taken any statistics courses prior to this class.
- *EA/YA/Career and Technical Education*: The learners in this computer class vary in their linguistic and academic abilities, as well as their state reading scores. The majority of students are in the "Basic" reading category which is below grade level. Four students are "Below Basic"

which signifies they are far below grade level. Only one student in the whole class is "Proficient" and on grade level. The class personality is pleasant and cooperative, and most students are generally on-task.

Keep these points in mind when describing.

- Be succinct. Say enough to paint the picture, then stop.
- Decide which facts and details are significant and emphasize those.
- Concentrate on facts and details that show an impact on teaching or learning.
- Resist the urge to tell *everything*. Details matter, but don't go on and on.
- Description should be the smallest part of your writing.
- Follow suggested page limits. They are there for a reason—to keep you from writing too much description and not enough analysis and reflection.
- Support descriptions with details and examples—but not too many.

Analysis Asks So What and Why?

Description is the writing style that tells *what*. Analysis is the writing style that asks *so what?* and *why?* Compare it to an attorney who puts forth a theory, then goes about confirming or rejecting it depending on the evidence. Teachers make hundreds of decisions each day that are implicit in their knowledge of their students and content area, but seldom need to express this minutia orally or in writing. However, the analysis questions in each entry require this intrinsic knowledge be put into words on paper. Analytical writing is important because

- It is the most evidentiary of the three styles.
- It demonstrates significance: *so what?* and *why?*
- It shows the assessor the reasons and motives (rationale) for your actions and decisions.
- It interprets and justifies actions and decisions—backed up with evidence.

- It shows the assessor the thought processes you used to reach decisions.
- It examines why elements or events are described in certain ways.
- It involves taking apart what occurred during a teaching event.

Prompts that ask for analysis may contain these key words:

- How?
- Why?
- In what ways . . . ?
- Tell your rationale for . . .
- Explain why . . .

What Works: Use These Sentence Starters for Analytical Responses:

- Because I know ___, I __ (planned, provided, organized, taught . . .), which shows . . .
- I chose ___ because . . .
- There are several reasons why . . .
- The ___ on his paper showed me that he didn't understand ___, so I . . .
- The rationale behind my decision to ___ was . . .
- This was significant because . . .
- This impacted student learning by . . .
- Because ___, therefore . . .
- In order to ___, I . . .

The subject(s) being analyzed (student work samples or a video) must be available and visible to the assessors. Clearly label your student work samples and/or video and refer to them in the text. Assessors will look at the student work samples and videos to compare them to the evidence in your analysis. Typically, the assessor reads your entry, looks at the work samples or video to see how they support your writing and "match up," and then may read the entry again. The analysis helps the assessors see the significance of the evidence you submit.

Reflection Asks Now What?

The descriptive style of writing tells *what*—like a witness giving testimony or a journalist. The analytical style asks *so what* and *why*, like an attorney questioning a witness or a scientist. The reflective style goes a step further and asks *now what?* Reflection is like a jury looking back at the evidence to decide a case or like a follow-up visit to a doctor to monitor a course of treatment. Reflection is a kind of self-analysis that

- Explains the thought processes used *after* teaching a lesson/unit.
- Tells how you would make decisions in the future.
- Is retrospective.
- Explains the significance of a decision.
- Tells the impact of a decision, activity, or action.
- Reviews instructional strategy choices.
- Sets new goals based on your analytical conclusions.
- Demonstrates your understanding of the National Board Standards.

Prompts that require reflection ask you to look back at your teaching practice and/or to look ahead and predict what you might do differently. Analysis and reflection often overlap. Reflective prompts may ask you to make a judgment about:

- What would you do differently if you were to teach the lesson again?
- What does the featured student's performance suggest about your teaching practice?
- Were these goals appropriate? Why?
- Were your lesson design, strategies, and materials appropriate? How do you know?
- How did students perform in light of the chosen goals?
- Could I have taken this a step further to increase student understanding?
- What did I learn from this experience that will help me do even better next time?
- What did I learn about my teaching practice in relation to student learning?

Reflection assumes that analysis has already taken place. A typical mistake teachers make is to *retell*, rather than *reflect*. When you reflect, you *explain* and *interpret* what happened, *then* tell what should come next. You look back, then forward.

Use These Pointers for Reflection:

- *Be honest.* There is always something that can be done better. No lesson is perfect.
- *Be realistic.* Don't propose something that is clearly impossible.
- *Focus* on both strengths and weaknesses of a lesson. No lesson is a total failure.
- *Use* concrete evidence to support your statements.
- *Align* and connect your instructional goals, the assessment activity, and your reflection on the lesson. There must be total consistency and agreement among them.
- *Focus* on the impact your teaching has had on your students.

What Works!

Use These Sentence Starters for Reflective Responses:

- In the future I . . .
- A key success was . . .
- An area for improvement is . . .
- My plan for the next lesson is . . .
- If I were to do this again . . .
- I learned ___ which will help me plan better next time by . . .
- Before this lesson my students . . . , but because of this experience . . .
- Because of this teaching experience, I learned . . .

Why These Work!

The boundaries between analysis and reflection are not always clear-cut. Analysis focuses on *so what?*, reflection focuses on *now what?* Analysis is about the past; reflection is about using the past to determine future actions. Understanding reflection will make your writing stronger.

Evidence or Lack of Evidence in Your Writing:

Read and reflect on the following samples to see if you can tell the difference in the amount of evidence presented in each pair of examples:

- **#1—Lack of Evidence**: Rory had trouble writing complete responses to comprehension questions, so I gave him a graphic organizer to help him organize his thoughts and information.
- **#1—With Evidence**: I planned a reading comprehension activity. I directed students to read a text and answer questions. Rory was unable to write responses in complete sentences, and he also skipped questions. To determine Rory's reading level, I administered the DAP (Developmental Reading Assessment). I learned he could answer questions orally but struggled to put his thoughts on paper. Rory shared that when he saw a list of questions he felt overwhelmed, so I began having him use a graphic organizer I designed that allowed him to record information in shortened form . . .
- **#2—Lack of Evidence**: My classroom is set up so kids can get their own supplies. One student from each group got supplies for their group. Each group set up their ramp and started rolling their cars down it to see how far they would travel. Marci's group rolled a car down their ramp and it traveled a yard. They knew this because they measured with their string and a yardstick.
- **#2—With Evidence**: I set up my science lab and centers for easy access to materials and to give adequate space for the inquiry activity. Marci was easily able to retrieve the materials her group needed to measure the distance their car rolled off their ramp. She and her group also had space to place their ramp and have room for the car to roll. When the car came to a stop, they used the string to measure from the bottom of the ramp to the front end of the car. Then they laid the string on a yardstick to measure the distance in inches and feet. Sam measured and declared the distance to be 3 feet. Lynn said, "That is a yard. Our car traveled a yard!" I asked others in the group if they agreed. Marci replied, "Yes, 3 feet is the same as a yard." This showed me everyone in that group understood the measuring equivalents.

- **#3—Lack of Evidence**: I used materials and realia from Mexico, Costa Rica, Spain, and Panama for this lesson to provide a more concrete visual of the foreign country.
- **#3—With Evidence**: I used a variety of authentic materials and realia for this lesson to provide a more concrete visual of the foreign country. My bulletin board was covered with a map of Mexico, pictures from a Costa Rican calendar, newspapers from Spain, posters from a travel company, photographs from books, and magazine ads promoting Panama as a tour destination.

What Works!

Give specific examples in your written commentary to give a clear, consistent, and convincing picture of your accomplished teaching. *EXAMPLES = EVIDENCE.*

Why This Works!

Examples build a strong wall of evidence!

Danger! Style Faux Pas and Pitfalls:

While learning to write with the three styles, some writing hazards emerge. Watch out for these and avoid them:

- ***Missing Person Alert*** Q: What is missing from this hypothetical passage?

    The students were introduced to their new vocabulary by using flashcards. After practicing as a whole group, they were divided into study groups. First they were assigned jobs within the group. Each group was provided with a set of flashcards and a worksheet to reinforce their learning. After all of the groups finished, we discussed the words again. Then each was assigned words to use in a sentence and illustrate.

    Q: *What is wrong with the above passage?*
    A: The teacher is missing! Nowhere in that passage is the teacher mentioned. Who is the teacher? Where is the teacher? When writing

your entries, don't hide in the background or be invisible. You must put yourself in the picture—clearly, consistently, and convincingly. How do you do that?

How to fix it: *Write in the first person!* *I* introduced students to their new vocabulary using flashcards. After practicing as a whole group, *I* divided them into study groups. First *I* assigned jobs within the group then *I* provided a set of flashcards and worksheet to reinforce their learning. After all of the groups finished, *I* led a discussion about the words and assigned words to use in a sentence and illustrate.

What Works! Making Yourself Visible Within Your Writing:

- Write in the first person. Use the pronoun *I* frequently. Candidates often feel that writing about themselves is bragging, and that feels uncomfortable. Put those feeling aside and use first-person pronouns in order to showcase your actions.
- Be careful with the pronoun **we**. It takes more space, but it is stronger to say the students and I rather than **we**. That way it's clear just who **we** are; *you* are in the picture.
- Use **we** sparingly. Use it once, then switch back to *I*.
- In Component 4, when using **we** to show collaboration, use it once, then turn the focus to your own contribution and switch to *I* or **my**: *I* collaborated with my department to plan the science fair. **We** each had assigned roles. **My** role was to . . .
- Use the active voice because it is clearer, more direct, and more concise. Go back and look at the example passage. Not only is the teacher missing, the verbs are almost all written in the passive voice. Sentences using passive voice verbs are wordier, longer, and less clear than those using the active voice. The *fixed* example uses active voice verbs.
- Use **helping verbs**, **by**, and **–ing** endings sparingly. For example, say: *I provided flashcards* . . . instead of *Flashcards were provided* . . . or *I was providing* . . . After writing a draft, go back and highlight each verb phrase with a helper and/or –ing. Then rewrite as many as possible in the active voice.

Look again at the rewritten passage with pronouns that put the teacher into the picture and with active voice verbs. Do you see the differences?

Why This Works!

This passage is much stronger because the teacher is clearly in the picture, and the active voice verbs show who performed the actions expressed. There are also details to demonstrate how this teacher's actions support the National Board Standards. This lets the assessor know who led the lesson and how the teacher produced learning.

More Writing Faux Pas and Pitfalls:

- **Preaching from the Pulpit**: This occurs when the candidate uses the written commentary as a soapbox. Avoid inserting personal views and frustrations about teaching into the written commentary. It is a waste of words and space. In a nutshell, accomplished teachers are able to demonstrate accomplished teaching and student learning in spite of difficulties and obstacles. Assessors score only *evidence* of accomplished teaching, so it is important to use words and space to demonstrate your evidence.

- **The E.S.P. Communicator**: When candidates don't explain their actions and decisions clearly, the assessor is left to connect the dots. Be careful not to assume that the reasons for choices are so obvious that no explanation is needed. Some candidates may be clear about what they **do**, but they may write ambiguously or not at all about the thinking processes that led them to a particular decision. This is a common pitfall, especially among more experienced candidates whose actions have become so intuitive and automatic that they no longer deliberately think about the reasons for their decisions. It may seem tedious or annoying to be pressed into the deeper thinking that the analysis and reflection sections require. But you must explain the thinking and decision making processes you applied to student work samples, videos, or other artifacts used in the entries. Never assume that an assessor will *see* evidence without an explanation. Explain your decisions and choices.

- **The Feelings Guru**: This candidate substitutes feelings for concrete evidence. Work to eliminate all *I believe, I feel, I tried,* and *I think* statements from your writing. Although teachers are very caring people, the National Board entries are not the place to lay out your personal teaching philosophy or beliefs. Statements such as *I believe* *all children can learn . . .* or *I feel that all students should . . .* , however true, are irrelevant to the process. The assessor looks for **evidence** of a teacher's effectiveness, but a teacher's philosophy is not a measurable piece of evidence. Assessors look for evidence in the form of specific examples, descriptions, analysis, reflection, and artifacts such as student work samples and videos. Avoid these pitfalls by returning to the trial lawyer analogy. You must present evidence clearly, convincingly, and consistently to the assessors who are the judge and jury.

- **Jargon**: It is the specialized language, words, and terms used within a profession. Use it sparingly. Too much educational jargon gets in the way of understanding. The best writing is plain, simple, easily understood language—the kind you use when you talk.

What Works! Using Strong Verbs, Strong Phrases, and Bloom's Taxonomy

Writing strong National Board entries does not require a fancy vocabulary. The assessors come from all fifty states, big cities, and small towns, and are teachers just like you. Ask yourself whether anyone, from anywhere, will understand what you wrote and you'll be on the right track.

Strong Verbs and Phrases describe accomplished teaching actions and qualities that have meaning within the National Board Certification process. They are words that help you showcase your teaching practice as described in the Standards. They are, for the most part, plain, strong verbs and descriptive phrases. Using these verbs and phrases in your writing can lend clarity and strength to your descriptions, analyses, and reflections. But the criteria for using them are authenticity and honesty. They must have meaning within the context of your teaching practice. Here are some examples:

- **Strong Verbs**: I encouraged, developed, designed, guided, supported, organized, facilitated, chose, chose to, selected, challenged, provided, gave, taught, engaged, demonstrated, learned, modeled, measured, asked, practiced, assigned, performed, contributed, impacted, influenced, instructed, questioned.
- **Strong Phrases**: students as risk-takers, ways of learning, learning community, lifelong learner, build self-esteem, promote student

understanding, appropriate assessment, constructive feedback, fairness, equity, goal-related, integrated learning, behavior intervention, active engagement/listening, high expectations, insightful questions, meaningful, learning goals, outcome-based, reluctant learner, on task, rich and in-depth, inclusion, productive classroom, cooperative groups, parent partnerships.

- **More Strong Phrases**: community involvement, collaboration, diverse perspectives, beyond the classroom, high expectations, problem-solving, real-world applications, rich variety of sources, student ownership, teacher as a learner, teaching strategies, unique learning needs, varied assessments, work collaboratively, standards-based, content-oriented, application, direct impact on student learning, I learned, I should have, now I understand, relevant characteristics, and motivational.
- *Bloom's Taxonomy* is one of the best references for finding effective verbs that indicate levels of learning and for planning appropriate lessons. Here is a recap (lowest to highest levels):
- *Remembering*: define, memorize, record, identify, label, list, locate, match, name, recall, spell, tell, state, underline, recognize, repeat
- *Understanding*: restate, discuss, describe, explain, express, identify, interpret, paraphrase, put in order, restate, retell, summarize, review
- *Applying*: apply, conclude, construct, use, dramatize, illustrate, show, sketch, draw, give a new example, solve, operate, practice, translate
- *Analyzing*: distinguish, analyze, differentiate, appraise, experiment, compare, contrast, diagram, debate, categorize, classify, dissect, infer
- *Evaluating*: defend, judge, value, evaluate, support, argue, appraise
- *Creating*: assemble, construct, create, design, develop, formulate, write

Why These Work!

These verbs provide evidence in your writing. They indicate your deliberate participation in the processes that make up accomplished teaching, and are examples of the "language" used in the Standards that shows evidence of accomplished teaching. Apply the litmus test to decide if something meets the criteria for being universally understood. There must be no confusion about the terms used in the written commentary. This is especially true for the names of programs or materials you or your school utilizes. Be sure to spell them out and give a brief explanation.

Examples:

- Career Ladder, a pay for performance program . . .
- NCTM, the National Council of Teachers of Mathematics

What Works! Creating a Writing Framework

- Make the case that you are an accomplished teacher by showing evidence of exemplary teaching. You are the lawyer. The assessors are the judge and jury.
- Connect the three styles of writing to the prompts: description, analysis, and reflection.
- Keep description to a minimum. Description tells *what*.
- Analysis asks *so what?* and *why?* and is the most evidentiary type of writing.
- Reflection asks *now what?* and is a type of self-analysis.
- Provide concrete examples of your actions and decisions.
- Write in the first person as much as possible.
- Use strong verbs and the active voice.
- Avoid using large amounts of educational jargon.
- Use buzz verbs, buzz phrases, and Bloom's Taxonomy language where appropriate.
- Be authentic.

Why These Work!

Your writing is the "legal brief" of your portfolio. It contains all the evidence to show the assessors that you are an accomplished teacher.

What Works! Following the 3Cs in the Level 4 Rubric:

- *Clear*: Never assume anything and explain everything.
- *Consistent*: Goals, activities, assessments, and so on must match up and be connected.
- *Convincing*: Build a wall of evidence with examples.

Add more Cs:

- *Concise*: Make your point and move on. Write short, to-the-point sentences.
- *Correct*: Use correct grammar and punctuation so the assessor can focus on your content.
- *Concrete*: Evidence needs to be specific, real, and measureable, not vague and ambiguous.

Style Tips:

- Limit bolding, underlining, and CAPS. A little goes a long way.
- Be as consistent as possible with verb tenses.
- Talk to the assessor, not at the assessor. The assessor is your audience.
- Write in your own voice. Don't lose yourself in the writing process.
- State the *significance* of events.
- Avoid acronyms unless you are sure the assessor will understand them or can explain them.
- Streamline writing and cut the fluff. Edit! Edit! Edit numerous times!
- Avoid *helping verbs* and *–ing* forms of verbs wherever possible.

Be Sure To:

- Back up your writing on your computer often!
- Pay attention to page limits. Assessors can read only the required number of pages.
- Answer *all* parts of every question/prompt. Respond *to* the question, not *about* it.

- Show impact on student learning.
- Connect your teaching practice to the Standards.
- Study the Architecture of Accomplished Teaching for insight into the prompts.
- Give up stressing about the vagueness of the prompts. It will only drive you crazy.

Why These Work!

Clear, consistent, convincing writing showcases your evidence.

7 Understanding Your Scores

Six-Word Memoir: National Board Certification—Best Professional Development
BOBBIE, AZ

The Scoring Process:

The National Board scoring process is the Gold Standard for fair assessment. Components 2–4 are submitted in mid-May. The C1 assessment window ends in mid-June. Assessors are all working teachers, and many are still teaching until mid-June, so no scoring can occur until then.

All assessors undergo rigorous training before any scoring can start. Some applicants are weeded out. Assessors are quality checked regularly DURING the scoring cycle to assure inter-rater reliability. The Selected Response items in C1 are machine-scored, but the Constructed Response items in Component 1 and Components 2, 3, and 4 cannot be machine-scored. These require careful human examination.

Once the scoring teams are set, components are scored from mid/late June through August. In every cycle, some submitted work requires extra scrutiny. Some work may be incomplete, incorrectly formatted, missing parts, suspected of plagiarism, or have any of several other issues. Any work that falls into that category is scored by an additional person, usually a supervisor. With 20,000+ candidates, the number of components needing special attention can be large. These all require extra time to sort through and be deemed complete. It's usually September, October, or maybe even November before these are resolved and finalized. Remember, everyone who scores is an actively working teacher, so the workforce is reduced because most scorers are back in school teaching. Most of the issues at this level are addressed by supervisors.

Scores must be inputted into the system, and a whole series of checks are conducted to assure that each and every score is first, correctly assessed, then entered into the system correctly. Statistical data are run to assure accuracy of every score and input.

All scoring and checking procedures must be complete before any score is released—scores can't be released piecemeal. So it's easily late November into December before every check, every step is complete and ready for release. There is even more to the process than I am aware of because I am not an assessor. It's a comprehensive, complex process, and there is always more than meets the eye.

Although it's hard to wait months for your score, we should all be glad it's so thorough because it ensures the highest degree of accuracy possible—which means that when you get your score, it will be correct. It's not ridiculous that all this takes time. You don't want to be the one whose score is rushed just so you can see it sooner. The process is designed for your benefit. Many professional certifications/licenses take considerable time to process, not just this one. I hope this explanation will help you better understand the scoring process and encourage you to take a deep breath and accept that you'll need to draw on your patience. The wait gives you time and space to find your way back to "normal" and get a positive start to your school year.

Specifics of the Process

No feedback statements are provided for Component 1. Standardized Feedback Statements are provided for Components 2, 3, and 4 if they receive a score below 3.75. The statements are directly connected to the Five Core Propositions AND the NB Standards. They are also connected to particular prompts (which are also connected to the Propositions and Standards) within each component. Your assessment is based on how strongly you show that you include the Propositions and Standards in your teaching practice. Language is **nuanced** among levels.

You Can Understand Your Scores

Scores designations encompass four levels numbered from 0 to 4. Each level has information and specific feedback statements to show the level of accomplishment demonstrated within each component. Statements are tailored to the content and rubric statements of each component, so they vary to some degree from component to component. However, all statements, across the components, have a common structure. Here is a general explanation of each level.

- **Level 0—NOT SCORABLE (NS)**: This score is the lowest and most serious score designation. Reasons can range from not submitting a component or not attending your assessment center appointment to being suspected of plagiarism. There are a number of other possible reasons for a "0." Refer to the Scoring Guide, page 7 for a more complete list.

- **Level 1**: Level 1 statements begin with the words, **You may wish to provide evidence of ___ . OR You may wish to focus on ___ .** This means evidence to address/support the prompts is severely lacking or missing altogether. The writing may have gotten seriously off track. *Evidence* can refer to specific examples/rationales within a prompt response and/or support for the writing in the form of student work samples (C2), video and instructional materials (C3), and KOS/Assessment/ PLN/SN data (C4). It can also indicate that prompts or parts of prompts, forms, or other sections of a component were missing.

- **Level 2:** A "2" is the most commonly received score among all candidates. Level 2 statements begin with the words: **You may wish to provide CLEARER evidence of/that___ .** This means you presented *SOME* evidence, but *MORE* was needed. Likely more specifics and/or rationales were needed. Writing may have been too general. Writing may not be clear or may not have been supported with specifics and/or rationales. There may have been inconsistencies. Evidence submitted might not have been tightly connected to the goals/lessons.

- **Level 3**: Level 3 statements begin with the words: **You may wish to provide more CONSISTENT and CONVINCING evidence of ___ .** This means you submitted ample evidence, but may have needed more/stronger specifics and/or rationales. There may have been minor inconsistencies. Note that any score in the 3-family is considered high and accomplished.

Components that receive a 3.75 or higher do not receive any feedback statements. The work is obviously accomplished.

What Works!

Notice the **progression/nuance** of language through the levels.

- Level 1: You may wish to focus on, *provide evidence* of/that, review instructions to ___.
- Level 2: You may wish to provide *clearer* evidence of/that ___.
- Level 3: You may wish to provide more *consistent and convincing* evidence of ___.

These are clues to help you understand where and how you could do better if you retake a component.

Why This Works!

Honing in on the nuances of the wording allows you to analyze and reflect on your previous submission to see where and how it could be strengthened.

What Works!

To be fully informed, it is imperative to read the Scoring Guide in its entirety. Every aspect of the scoring process is explained. A comprehensive understanding of the process serves to inform and enhance your work to lead to certification.

Appendix A
SSTARS Lesson Plan Template Based on the Architecture of Accomplished Teaching

Table A.1 SSTARS Lesson Plan Template

STUDENTS (Step 1: Knowledge of Students) WHAT I KNOW ABOUT: • These students at this time, in this setting • Learning styles • Abilities • Needs • Prior Knowledge	
SET GOALS (Step 2: Set high, worthwhile goals) • Goals • Objectives • Activities • Unifying Concepts/Big Ideas	
TEACH (Step 3: Implement instruction) • Appropriate strategies • Activities support goals • Appropriate pacing	
ASSESS (Step 4: Evaluate learning in light of the goals) • Monitor progress purposefully • Assess throughout the lesson sequence • Observations • Informal • Formal • Remediate/Enrich	
REFLECT (Step 5: Reflect on student learning) • Effectiveness • Successes • Modification	
START AGAIN (Step 6: Set new high, worthwhile goals) • For these students, at this time, in this setting	

Appendix B
Sentence Stems for Analytic and Reflective Writing

- I chose ___ because ___.
- The rationale behind my decision was ___.
- Because I know ___, I ___.
- The __ on his paper showed me ___, so I ___.
- First I ___, then I followed up by ___.
- This was significant because ___.
- When I saw ___, I realized ___.
- In order to ___, I ___.
- The reasons I chose ___ were ___.
- I used a variety of strategies including ___, ___, and ___.
- I saw the error was caused by ___, so I ___.
- As a result of ___, Jennifer was able to ___.

Appendix C
Ten Editing Tips to Trim Space without Trimming Content

1. **Turn off "widow/orphan" control.** This prevents a single line of a paragraph from being at the top of a new page. You'll save several lines in the space of an entry.
2. **Set to auto-hyphenate.** This will break words at the ends of lines to properly hyphenate. Saving even a few spaces on each page can help.
3. **Use contractions.** They save several spaces each time you use them. Word has an auto-correct feature called "Find and Replace." You may need to do this for each contraction.
4. **Use numerals instead of numbers.** You can break the rule you learned in school. Use numerals such as 12 instead of twelve and 6th instead of sixth.
5. **Start your commentary on the same line as the heading.** Example: Video Analysis: This lesson features eighty-nine twenty-five 1st graders learning to sharpen pencils.
6. **Make sure your candidate number is in a header, not in the body.**
7. **Find and replace the period-double-space.** This is a big space saver over the length of a component.
8. **Take *the*, *my*, and *that* out of most sentences.** The meaning won't change, but and you'll gain space.
9. **Remove as many adjectives and adverbs as possible. Replace: She writes with vivid and inspired word choice . . .** with **She writes with strong word choice . . .**
10. **Eliminate paragraphs. Bold the first word or two of each new response** as a visual aid to the assessor. If you use paragraphs, indent 2 or 3 spaces instead of the usual 5 spaces.

About the Author

Bobbie Faulkner spent thirty-eight years teaching grades K-6 in public schools in Ohio, Kentucky, and Arizona. She is certified as a Middle Childhood Generalist and has renewed her certification. She has supported candidates in all certification areas for almost two decades and has mentored candidates in her home district and state, as well as in university and regional cohorts. She offers webinars to districts and cohorts on National Board topics. Bobbie can be contacted at nbwhatworks@gmail.com.